Arms and legs, fingers and toes

Bobbie Kalman

🌤 Crabtree Publishing Company

www.crabtreebooks.com

Created by Bobbie Kalman

Author and Editor-in-Chief
Bobbie Kalman

Educational consultants
Elaine Hurst
Joan King
Reagan Miller

Editors
Reagan Miller
Joan King
Kathy Middleton

Proofreader
Crystal Sikkens

Design
Bobbie Kalman
Katherine Berti

Photo research
Bobbie Kalman

Production coordinator
Katherine Berti

Prepress technician
Katherine Berti

Photographs by Shutterstock

Library and Archives Canada Cataloguing in Publication

Kalman, Bobbie, 1947-
    Arms and legs, fingers and toes / Bobbie Kalman.

(My world)
ISBN 978-0-7787-9416-5 (bound).--ISBN 978-0-7787-9460-8 (pbk.)

    1. Extremities (Anatomy)--Juvenile literature.
I. Title. II. Series: My world (St. Catharines, Ont.)

QL548.K34 2010   j612'.98   C2009-906051-5

Library of Congress Cataloging-in-Publication Data

Kalman, Bobbie.
    Arms and legs, fingers and toes / Bobbie Kalman.
        p. cm. -- (My world)
    ISBN 978-0-7787-9460-8 (pbk. : alk. paper) -- ISBN 978-0-7787-9416-5
(reinforced library binding : alk. paper)
    1. Extremities (Anatomy)--Juvenile literature. I. Title. II. Series.

    QM548.K28 2010
    612.7'5--dc22
                                                        2009040953

Crabtree Publishing Company

www.crabtreebooks.com   1-800-387-7650

Printed in China/122009/CT20091009

Published in Canada
Crabtree Publishing
616 Welland Ave.
St. Catharines, Ontario
L2M 5V6

Published in the United States
Crabtree Publishing
PMB 59051
350 Fifth Avenue, 59th Floor
New York, New York 10118

Published in the United Kingdom
Crabtree Publishing
Maritime House
Basin Road North, Hove
BN41 1WR

Published in Australia
Crabtree Publishing
386 Mt. Alexander Rd.
Ascot Vale (Melbourne)
VIC 3032

Words to know

fingers

arm

hand

leg

knee

toes

foot

ankle

fist

thumb

wrist

elbow

3

feet

The boy is standing on his feet.

toes

The girl is standing on her toes.

legs

The girl is walking on her legs.

ankle

The boy is holding the ball with his ankle.

— knee

The boy is bending his knees.

wrist

The baby is bending her wrists.

hands

The children are holding hands.

fist

The girl is punching with her fist.

finger

The boy is pointing his finger up.

thumb

The girl is pointing her thumbs up.

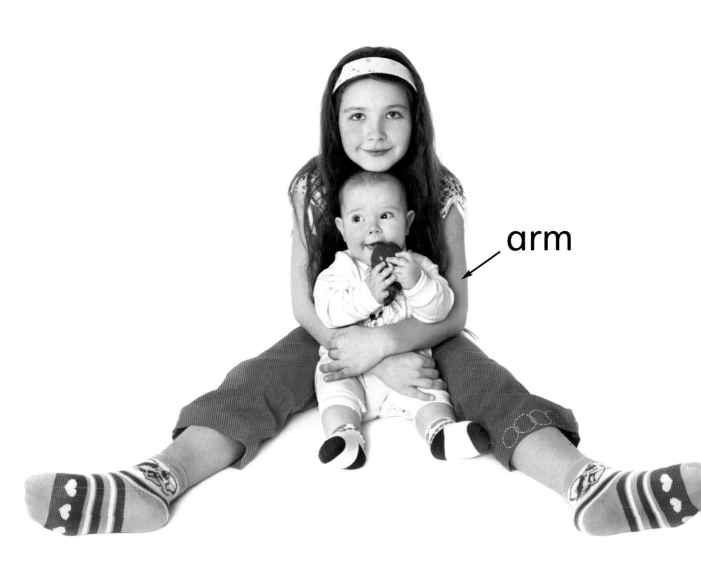

arm

The girl is holding a baby in her arms.

elbows

The boys are leaning on their elbows.

Notes for adults

How do they move?

Arms and legs, fingers and toes looks at the parts of a child's limbs that move. It introduces verbs of movement that are related to using each part, such as crawling, walking, standing, sitting, bending, holding, leaning, pointing, and so on.

Rewrite the song!

Ask children to move their arms, fingers, or feet in different ways and have other children guess each action. Then ask them to name two or more actions that a person could do with each body part, such as touching or stroking with fingers, throwing or holding with hands, and walking or kicking with feet. The children can help rewrite the song "Head and shoulders, knees, and toes" using the words from this book. They can then sing the new song while pointing to those body parts. What fun!

Simon Says

Play a game of "Simon Says." This active game helps children identify their body parts and explore different ways each body part can move. It also helps children practice following directions. Simon Suggestions: Simon says...put your hands on your knees, wave your hands in the air, touch elbows with a friend, hop on one foot, point one thumb up and one thumb down, and so on. Children can take turns leading the game.